DELICIOUS

The Life & Art of Wayne Thiebaud

DELICIOUS

BY SUSAN GOLDMAN RUBIN

chronicle books · san francisco

To Martin, Cooper, Jake, Max, and Olivia —S. G. R.

Acknowledgments:
First and foremost I thank Wayne Thiebaud for generously giving me so much of his time and thoughtfully answering questions. I also thank his son Paul LeBaron Thiebaud for opening his gallery to me and helping me choose the art for this book. A special thank-you to Colleen Casey, director of LeBaron's Fine Art in Sacramento, California, for her patience and dedication. I am grateful to my editor, Victoria Rock, for enthusiastically believing in this project right from the start, and to her assistant, Melissa Manlove. My thanks to Robert Panzer and Paula Mazzotta of the Visual Artists and Galleries Association (VAGA) for their cooperation. And of course, a huge bouquet of thanks to my agent and mentor, George Nicholson, who urged me on when I expressed a passionate desire to do this book. Thanks also to his assistant, Thaddeus Bower. As always, I am grateful to my friends at Lunch Bunch and to the Thursday night group for listening and critiquing. And lastly, I thank my husband, Michael, for supporting my research and sharing tennis talk with Wayne Thiebaud.

All works of art by Wayne Thiebaud are © Wayne Thiebaud, licensed by VAGA, New York, NY.
Three Machines: Museum purchase, Walter H. and Phyllis J. Shorenstein Foundation Fund, the Roscoe and Margaret Oakes Income Fund, with additional funds from Claire E. Flagg, the Museum Society Auxiliary, Mr. and Mrs. George R. Roberts, Mr. and Mrs. John N. Rosekrans, Jr., Mr. and Mrs. Robert Bransten, Mr. and Mrs. Steven MacGregor Read, and Bobbie and Mike Wilsey, from the Morgan Flagg Collection, 1993.18

Book design by Jennifer Olsen, Paper Plane Studio.
Typeset in Beton Demi and Gotham Bold.
Manufactured by Midas Printing Ltd., Boluo Yuanzhou, China, in April 2010.

Library of Congress Cataloging-in-Publication Data
Rubin, Susan Goldman.
Delicious : the life and art of Wayne Thiebaud / by Susan Goldman Rubin.
p. cm.
Includes bibliographical references and index.
ISBN-13: 978-0-8118-5168-8
ISBN-10: 0-8118-5168-0
1 Thiebaud, Wayne. 2. Painters—United States—Biography. 3. Desserts in art.
I. Title. II. Title: Life and art of Wayne Thiebaud.
ND237.T5515R83 2007
759.13—dc22
[B]
2006031168

10 9 8 7 6 5 4 3 2

This product conforms to CPSIA 2008.
Chronicle Books LLC
680 Second Street, San Francisco, California 94107

www.chroniclekids.com

As I began researching *Delicious*, I hoped I would have a chance to interview Wayne Thiebaud in person. Just in case, I carefully prepared a list of questions and brought it along when I flew to Sacramento, where Wayne lives.

I had arranged to spend the day at LeBaron's Fine Art gallery, owned and run by Wayne's son Paul. The Thiebaud family wanted me to consider using paintings, pastels, and prints for this book that had not been previously or widely published. I sat down at a lightbox and happily started viewing about 200 transparencies of Wayne's art.

During the morning, I met Paul, who said that his dad would probably not stop by after playing his daily game of tennis. But I kept my hopes up. Then, while I was deeply absorbed in studying transparencies and taking notes, in walked Wayne Thiebaud. Paul introduced us. Wayne is tall, friendly, and soft spoken. I was so excited and flustered that I forgot to whip out my list of interview questions. Wayne sat down on the other side of the desk and we talked face-to-face. After half an hour he said he had to leave. But I still had more questions! Wayne kindly allowed me to send them by e-mail and he recorded his answers on a cassette tape.

On the trip home I flew over Wayne's beloved Sacramento River Delta. Looking down I could see the landscape through his eyes. The experience of interviewing him in person had greatly enriched my understanding and enjoyment of his art. I am happy to be able to share that pleasure with you.

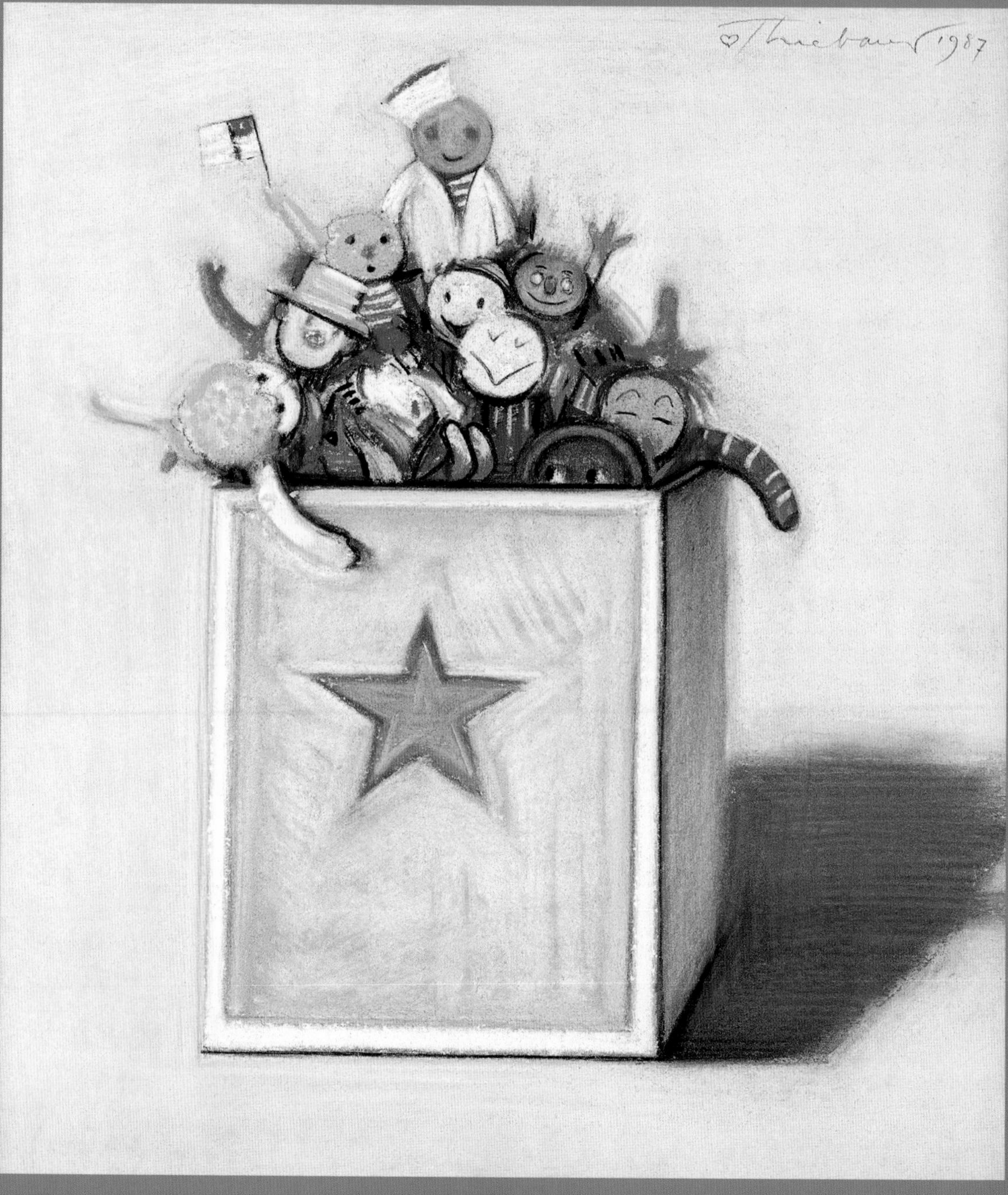
Thiebaud 1987

A GREAT WAY TO GROW UP

DOLL BOX, 1987, PASTEL ON BOARD, 10³/₄ X 9¹/₄ INCHES, PRIVATE COLLECTION

Wayne Thiebaud loves food, especially desserts. Not only does he enjoy eating cakes, pies, and cupcakes, he also paints pictures of them. The word that best describes his art is . . .

"DELICIOUS."

Wayne paints these pictures from his memories, mostly from childhood. He remembers family picnics with tables piled high with homemade food. His mother, Alice, was a wonderful cook and baker. On rainy days she set up art projects for Wayne and his younger sister, Marjory Jean. Sometimes their uncle Jess, a cartoonist, came over and drew funny pictures for them. Wayne decided he wanted to be a cartoonist, too. He never dreamed that one day he would become one of the best-known American painters of the twentieth century.

WAYNE THIEBAUD IN HIS STUDIO AT ROSEBUD FARM, HOOD, CALIFORNIA, ca 1968, PHOTO BY BETTY JEAN THIEBAUD, THIEBAUD FAMILY COLLECTION

Wayne grew up in the American West. He was born on November 15, 1920, in Mesa, Arizona. When he was one year old, the family moved to Long Beach, California.

"I WAS A SPOILED CHILD. I HAD A GREAT LIFE, SO ABOUT THE ONLY THING I CAN DO IS TO PAINT HAPPY PICTURES."

—WAYNE THIEBAUD

During the summers he visited his grandfather's little farm in Southern California. His grandfather, a retired schoolteacher, grew experimental crops. As Wayne did chores he became fascinated by the patterns of the crops. And he stored these patterns in his mind.

WAYNE THIEBAUD, 1924, LONG BEACH, CALIFORNIA, THIEBAUD FAMILY COLLECTION

THE RIVERHOUSE, 2001, OIL ON CANVAS, 18 X 35³⁄₄ INCHES, PRIVATE COLLECTION, SACRAMENTO

In 1931 Wayne's family moved to southern Utah. His father had given up his job as a mechanic and had leased a big ranch to take up farming. Wayne, now 11 years old, helped with the farmwork. He hitched up teams of horses to the plow and furrowed the soil. He planted alfalfa, potatoes, and corn, and harvested the crops.

The Thiebauds were Mormons, and the church played an important part in their lives. "I grew up a good Mormon boy," said Wayne. From an early age he followed his parents' example of honesty and hard work. His grandmother on his mother's side had been one of the first Mormon pioneers who had settled in Utah in the mid-1800s. Her last name was LeBaron. Wayne's father was a bishop in the Mormon Church. "I was exposed to discussion," said Wayne. "The spit and argue club. I was fascinated by that."

In 1933, when Wayne was 13 years old, his family moved back to Long Beach. His father no longer had enough money to pay for the ranch, and they lost it. These were the years known as the Great Depression in America. Families throughout the country lost their homes, jobs, and savings.

Wayne helped his family earn money by working in cafés on the Long Beach boardwalk. When he was about 14 he had a job washing dishes at a stand that sold hot dogs, hamburgers, and ice cream. One day Wayne's boss promoted him from dishwasher to cook. At first Wayne was pleased. Then the boss gave him a bag of pancake flour and told him to mix it with the ground meat to make it go further. Wayne refused to trick the customers, so he quit. But images of hamburgers, hot dogs, and ice-cream cones stayed with him.

At Long Beach Polytechnic High School, Wayne played basketball and football, and also became active in the theater department. His theater arts teacher took the students behind the scenes at a real theater, the Pasadena Playhouse. There, they learned about the dramatic effects of lighting and stage design. Wayne was struck by the shadows that actors made when they were lit by stage light.

Wayne didn't realize it, but he was collecting images and storing them to use in his paintings later.

"OBJECTS ARE FOR ME LIKE . . . CHARACTERS IN A PLAY."

—WAYNE THIEBAUD

HAMBURGER, 1961, OIL ON CANVAS, 12 X 16¼ INCHES, COLLECTION OF PAUL LEBARON THIEBAUD

FROM CARTOONS TO PAINTING

TOY MICKEY, 1988, OIL ON WOOD, 12⅛ X 12⅛ INCHES, PRIVATE COLLECTION

WAYNE THIEBAUD WORKING ON *ALECK* CARTOONS, 1944, MATHER ARMY AIR FIELD, THIEBAUD FAMILY COLLECTION

Wayne broke his back playing football in his junior year of high school. While he was recuperating he kept himself busy by drawing.

"THE MORE I DREW, THE MORE I IMPROVED."

—WAYNE THIEBAUD

He especially loved cartooning. He became so skillful that to this day he can draw Popeye with both hands at the same time. He draws cartoons every day and collects original American cartoons from the 1920s and 1930s.

While still in high school Wayne landed a job in the animation department at Walt Disney Studios. Like other young artists at Disney, he learned to do what was called "in-between" drawings. In-betweeners sketched the action that came between the main movements of the cartoon characters. Wayne did in-betweens of Goofy, Pinocchio, and Jiminy Cricket. "I was sixteen years old and making fourteen dollars a week," he said proudly, "working about sixty hours a week and going to school."

Fourteen dollars was a lot of money in those days. In 1936 a quart of milk cost 11 cents, a can of soup was a dime, and a nickel bought a candy bar or bottle of soda.

Wayne wanted to go to art school. But he didn't have enough money for tuition. So he presented his drawings at the Frank Wiggins Trade School in Los Angeles where tuition was free. He was accepted. One of his two teachers illustrated advertisements for clothes and shoes. He taught Wayne skills that came in handy.

Wayne earned money illustrating movie posters, painting and lettering signs, and occasionally selling his cartoons.

When the United States entered World War II, Wayne joined the air force. He was 22 and wanted to become a pilot. However, he wound up as an army artist instead. He created a cartoon strip called *Aleck* for the newspaper at his army base. And he designed posters and painted murals. While he was in the army Wayne married Patricia Patterson, and they had a daughter, Twinka.

When the war ended in 1945, Wayne decided to try to make a living as a cartoonist and commercial artist. His family stayed in Los Angeles while he went to New York to find work.

He lived at the YMCA and tried to sell his cartoons to magazines without success. Wayne had better luck getting a few assignments to draw illustrations for fashion magazines. The commercial artists he worked for liked him. They took time out to teach him new skills. "A lot of kind people in commercial art helped me," he said. "I learned so much! Like how to sharpen your pencil and all these really basic things." One art director took him aside and told him, "'You make the most ugly wash [ink or paint diluted with water] I've ever seen. Let me show you how to make a wash.' And sure enough," said Wayne, "she set up her board and showed me." Another thing Wayne learned to do was to work quickly. Instead of drawing a large, detailed picture right away, Wayne made what were called thumbnails. Thumbnails were little sketches or roughs that were done quickly to plan the whole picture.

"I LEARNED . . . HOW TO . . . DO THEM FROM MEMORY."
—WAYNE THIEBAUD

Without knowing it, Wayne was learning skills that he'd use later as a painter.

SHOE ROWS, 1975, OIL ON CANVAS, 30 X 24 INCHES, PRIVATE COLLECTION, SAN FRANCISCO

He wasn't getting anywhere as a cartoonist, though. And he missed his family in California. Soon he returned and settled with his wife and daughter in Los Angeles. Wayne went to work at the Rexall Drug Company as an art director and cartoonist, designing pages of the company's employee magazine. He also created a comic strip for the magazine that featured a little boy named Ferbus.

Around this time Wayne became seriously interested in fine art. He studied the work of great painters such as Michelangelo and Peter Paul Rubens to better understand illustrating. These painters had brilliantly captured the human figure on canvas and paper.

> "WHAT I COULDN'T GET OVER,
> WAS THAT ALL THE ILLUSTRATORS
> AND COMMERCIAL ARTISTS I ADMIRED MOST
> WERE CRAZY ABOUT THE OLD MASTERS."
>
> —WAYNE THIEBAUD

One illustrator Wayne admired was Robert Mallary. Mallary worked at Rexall to support himself as a painter. He and Wayne became friends, and Mallary introduced Wayne to painting. He gave Wayne art books to read and critiqued his work.

"HE WAS A MENTOR WHO TORE APART WHAT I DID."

—WAYNE THIEBAUD

But Wayne welcomed criticism that would improve his work. With Mallary's help, Wayne began showing his paintings in galleries. One of Wayne's pictures was chosen for an exhibit at the Los Angeles County Museum of Art. The experience thrilled him. Now he knew that he wanted to be a painter. All the skills he had stored up were about to be put to use.

RESERVOIR AND ORCHARD, 2001, ACRYLIC AND OIL ON CANVAS, 40 X 40 INCHES, PRIVATE COLLECTION, SACRAMENTO

BRUSH DANCE

STUFFED TOYS, 1996-2002, OIL ON CANVAS, 64 X 54 INCHES, COLLECTION OF GARY SUMERS, NEW YORK

TWO ROWS OF BOW TIES, 1969, PASTEL ON PAPER, 10³/₈ X 20⁷/₈ INCHES, PRIVATE COLLECTION

In 1949, Wayne decided he wanted to earn a college degree so that he could teach art. But would he be able to find a job when he graduated? Wayne made a daring decision. He left his job and went back to school. Because he was a veteran, the army paid for his school.

Wayne did not have to take the usual studio art classes because he had been drawing for so many years. And now he was also painting. So he mainly studied art history and education.

In 1951 Wayne graduated and got a job teaching at Sacramento Junior College. One of his students, Mel Ramos, recalled the first time he saw Wayne speak. It was at Ramos's high school on Career Day. Wayne talked about careers in commercial art. Ramos had taken an art class and made posters for high school events. He was impressed by what Wayne had said and what he wore—a purple corduroy jacket and a green bow tie. "He was just what I thought an artist should look like," remembered Ramos, who became Wayne's close friend and a well-known Pop artist and teacher himself.

In his classes, the first thing Wayne had his students focus on was drawing. He wanted them to learn to observe more carefully. He would tell his class to draw the same object over and over again with pencil and paper.

"DRAW TILL YOU GET IT RIGHT."

—WAYNE THIEBAUD

"What is the light source? Where is it coming from? What is its direction? It's a very complex problem to reduce the three-dimensional world to a two-dimensional surface." Sometimes Wayne's students would spend as much as four weeks drawing a single object. It was hard work.

"It was the most rigorous class I'd ever taken," recalled Jack Ogden, a student from Wayne's first Beginning Drawing class in the fall of 1951.

When Wayne's students were ready to move on to color and painting, he told them to do what he had done: copy the masters. Wayne would put a reproduction of a great painting on an easel next to his own and borrow ideas. After all, he faced some of the same challenges that other artists had been facing for centuries. "It is a joy to try to be part of the long and enduring tradition of the language of vision," he said. "I'm a dedicated museum-goer."

"I LOVE ART HISTORY."

—WAYNE THIEBAUD

TWO PAINT CANS, 1987, OIL ON PAPER, 13³/₄ X 20 INCHES, PRIVATE COLLECTION,
COURTESY OF LEBARON'S FINE ART, SACRAMENTO

In 1951, the year he started teaching, Wayne went back to school to earn his master's degree. The following year his second daughter, Mallary Ann, was born. She was named for Wayne's old friend and mentor, Robert Mallary.

Despite Wayne's busy schedule—teaching, studying, and spending time with his family—he devoted as much time as he could to painting in his studio. He experimented with a variety of media: oil, watercolor, and pastel. In those days there were no art galleries in Sacramento. So Wayne and his friends exhibited wherever they could—in restaurants, paint stores, and furniture stores. Once, he displayed his artwork in the snack bar of the Star-Lite Drive-In. Drive-ins were outdoor movie theaters popular in the 1950s. People drove in at dusk and stayed in their cars to watch the movie on a giant screen. The sound came from speakers that clipped onto car windows. Wayne hung his pictures in the area where popcorn and drinks were sold. In exchange, he received free tickets to the movie. However, Wayne wanted to show his work in a more suitable place—a real art gallery. Maybe even a gallery in New York City.

At that time the most critically acclaimed painters were based in New York. A group of them were called Abstract Expressionists. Painters such as Willem de Kooning and Franz Kline created wild pictures with energetic slashes and drips of paint to express their feelings. Wayne longed to find out more about them firsthand. Each year he organized trips to New York so students and faculty could visit galleries and museums. And in 1956 he took a year off from teaching and went to stay in New York. He earned money by working for advertising agencies. But his real interest was painting.

In the evenings Wayne sat in on discussions at the Cedar Street Bar, where artists gathered to talk. "They were wonderful discussions," said Wayne. He particularly admired Dutch-born de Kooning and met him at his studio. "De Kooning was very approachable," said Wayne, "very kind." De Kooning generously encouraged Wayne, as he did many younger artists. He, too, came from a background in commercial art. Like Wayne, he loved the physical act of painting. He showed Wayne what brushes he used. His brushstrokes had a kind of tempo, or rhythm.

THREE MACHINES, 1963, OIL ON CANVAS, 30 X 36½ INCHES, FINE ARTS MUSEUMS OF SAN FRANCISCO

PINBALL MACHINE, 1956, MIXED MEDIA ON MASONITE, 36 X 48 INCHES, PRIVATE COLLECTION

Wayne coined the term "brush dance" to describe the jumps and swirls of de Kooning's paint: "Very slow and very fast, very happy and very blue, all within a single picture."

Wayne's painting *Pinball Machine* in 1956 shows de Kooning's influence. Smears and drips of paint make it hard to clearly see the pinball and gum-ball machines. Wayne wanted to make his pictures "look like art." But he realized that he had covered up the objects with "arty strokes" because he felt embarrassed about painting such silly things.

Yet these were the things he really wanted to paint. Would he ever find his own way of painting them, his own brush dance?

LAYERS BENEATH THE LAYER CAKE

GUM MACHINE, 1964, PASTEL OVER HARDGROUND ETCHING, 12 X 8 INCHES,
COLLECTION OF PAUL LEBARON THIEBAUD

Over the next few years, Wayne kept painting. He revisited themes and made his pictures simpler, clearer. He did new drawings and paintings of things he liked: pies, hot dogs, cups of coffee, plates of bacon and eggs, club sandwiches, and penny machines full of gum balls and candy.

After he did his first picture of a row of pies, he sat down and laughed. Would people think he had "flipped out" or gone crazy? He believed that this new work would probably end his career as an artist. But he enjoyed what he was doing. He brought to his food paintings all the skills he had stored up.

When he composed his pictures he made a thumbnail sketch first. The thumbnails were small, about 2 inches by 3 inches. He played with ideas of how to arrange the objects in his picture. Wayne worked entirely from memory. He remembered the hot dogs, hamburgers, and ice-cream cones on the Long Beach boardwalk. "This is mostly the food every American child has been brought up on," he said. Wayne remembered family picnics with homemade pies and cakes. "Cakes, they are glorious, they are like toys." Wayne painted with thick brush strokes. Swirls of white, pink, lemon, and chocolate brown in *Four Cupcakes* (page 48) look like the frosting itself.

FOUR CUPCAKES, 1971, OIL ON PAPER MOUNTED ON CANVAS, 11 X 19¼ INCHES,
THIEBAUD FAMILY COLLECTION

PIE SLICE, 1991, OIL ON BOARD, 11½ x 14 INCHES, COLLECTION OF CROSBY AND BEBE KEMPER

Wayne saw the foods as geometric shapes. "When you think of it, [a slice of] pie is just a triangle," he explained. "Cakes are circles. I am interested in very, very basic shapes—circles, triangles, half-circles, rectangles."

Four Pinball Machines combines all of these shapes. Compared with his earlier painting *Pinball Machine* (page 42), details like knobs, handles, and decorative stars can be plainly seen. Gorgeous yellows, oranges, and lavenders delight the eye, unlike the muddy browns of his previous version.

To create bright color, Wayne hit on the idea of outlining shapes like the cupcakes in vivid blues and greens. The "rainbow" edges came about accidentally. Wayne's method of starting a painting was to sketch in the shapes in a light color, such as yellow. Then he went back and added deeper colors. As he layered the paint some of the color underneath remained as outlines and he found that he liked these "halos." At last he had developed a style of painting that was uniquely his.

During this period, Wayne also developed something else: he and his friends opened a cooperative art gallery in Sacramento where they could show their work—*without* movies and popcorn.

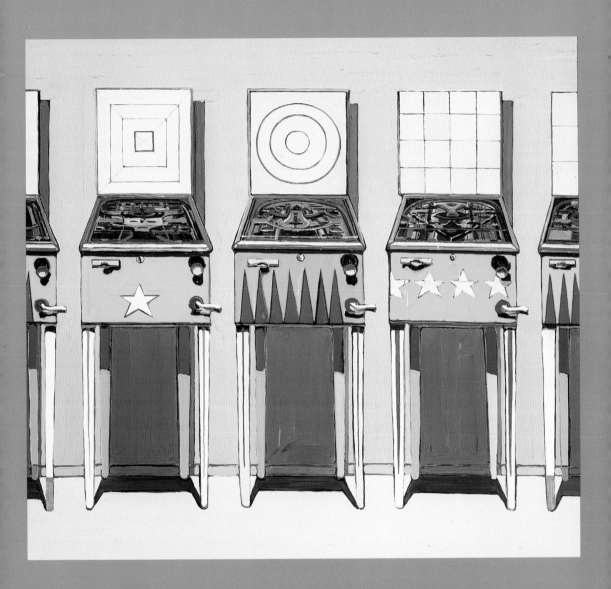

FOUR PINBALL MACHINES, 1962, OIL ON CANVAS, 67½ X 72 INCHES, PRIVATE COLLECTION

LONG SUCKERS, 1997, OIL ON BOARD, 12 X 18 INCHES, PRIVATE COLLECTION

There had been changes in Wayne's personal life, too. He and Patricia had divorced. In 1959 he married Betty Jean Carr and adopted her son, Matthew Bult. In 1960 their son, Paul LeBaron, was born. That same year Wayne was appointed assistant professor of art at California State University, Davis. His teaching schedule was a little lighter now and gave him more time for painting.

By 1961, after completing more than 100 drawings, paintings, and sketches, Wayne felt ready to show his work to the public. His first exhibit at the Artists Cooperative Gallery in Sacramento was a dud. People expected to see Wayne's old style of landscapes and figures. They were disappointed. Very few paintings were bought. Next, Wayne had a one-man show of his food paintings in a small San Francisco gallery. Nothing sold.

A critic wrote that Wayne must be

"THE HUNGRIEST ARTIST IN CALIFORNIA."

Discouraged but not defeated, Wayne decided to try New York. He and his friend and former student Mel Ramos drove across the country in the summer of 1961. Once in New York, Wayne plodded along from gallery to gallery showing his work, but no dealer wanted to represent him. Paintings of cakes, ice-cream cones, and lollipops seemed out of place in the world of abstract art. Wayne worked his way uptown, block by block. His last stop late one afternoon was the Allan Stone Gallery. The gallery represented Wayne's old friend Robert Mallary, who had encouraged him to go there.

Wayne trudged in carrying two rolls of paintings under his arms. Exhausted, he leaned against the doorway and said to Allan Stone, "You won't be interested in my work. Nobody else is."

Allan said, "You look like you need to sit down and take it easy. Let's go out for a hamburger. I know a great place."

Allan took Wayne to one of his favorite restaurants, the Embers, and they listened to jazz while they ate and talked. Allan asked Wayne to leave his paintings with him for a while, promising to send them back by parcel post. Wayne agreed and returned to Sacramento.

Allan's way of deciding what work to show was to bring it home, look at it, and live with it. He studied Wayne's ice cream, cakes, and rows of pies. "At first I thought they were kind of silly," he said, "but I couldn't get them out of my head. The stuff is serious stuff. There are layers beneath the layer cakes . . . I lived with Thiebaud's paintings for a month, and his images began to haunt me."

"WAYNE THIEBAUD IS THE PAINTER I WISH I COULD BE."

—ALLAN STONE

Finally Allan called Wayne and offered him a one-man show. Wayne was astonished. The show opened in April 1962 to rave reviews. East Coast critics recognized Wayne as a great new talent. Everything was sold. Many paintings were bought by museums and important private collectors.

From that day on, Allan represented Wayne, and the two remained close friends.

Thiebaud 1965   Paul 5 years

POSING FOR POP

PAUL AGED 5 YEARS, 1965, CHARCOAL ON PAPER, 10 X 9¼ INCHES, COLLECTION OF PAUL LEBARON THIEBAUD

FIVE ROWS OF SUNGLASSES, 2000, OIL ON CANVAS, 30 X 24 INCHES, PRIVATE COLLECTION

Wayne now had a gallery in New York where he could show his work. But would he hold his own as he competed with other artists? Wayne's success in 1962 came just when another new painter hit the New York art scene. His name was Andy Warhol. Critics called Warhol's paintings Pop Art, which meant art that was based on products and messages from popular culture. Warhol, like Wayne, came from a background in advertising. He painted pictures of ordinary food items, such as cans of Campbell's soup and bottles of Coca-Cola. Since Wayne also did paintings of prepared food, critics linked them together. But Wayne did not want to be lumped with Warhol and other Pop artists. He felt that Warhol's images were flat, mechanical paintings designed like billboards to quickly grab viewers' attention.

Wayne, on the other hand, followed a tradition of realist painting. He wanted to portray real things clearly and with feeling.

"I TRY TO FIND THINGS TO PAINT WHICH I FEEL HAVE BEEN OVERLOOKED."

—WAYNE THIEBAUD

He painted cakes, pies, and a whole bakery case full of desserts. He painted deli counters displaying salads, salamis, and cheeses. From food he branched out into other inanimate objects: balls, stuffed toys, high-heeled shoes, eyeglasses, yo-yos, and a doll box.

Wayne experimented with a variety of media in making pictures of the same subject. He portrayed cakes in oil paint, watercolor, and pastels. He even tried printmaking techniques. "All of them are interesting," he said. A lithograph titled *Display Rows* shows assorted desserts in shimmering colors.

To make a lithograph Wayne drew directly on stone. Then the image was printed on paper in black and white. Often he kept his prints around the studio and later reworked them by using crayons, pastels, watercolor, tempera, oil, and acrylic. "Surprising results occurred," he said. What happened to the pattern when the color changed? Did it improve the picture? Convey a different mood? Wayne has always been curious about how an image changes when it's rendered in color or black and white.

DISPLAY ROWS, 1990, COLOR LITHOGRAPH, 28³/₄ X 22³/₄ INCHES,
COURTESY OF PAUL THIEBAUD GALLERY, SAN FRANCISCO

RABBIT, 1966, PASTEL ON PAPER, 15 X 20 INCHES, PRIVATE COLLECTION

In 1963 Wayne returned to a more traditional painting subject: people. Painting people had always interested him. "My very first oil painting was a figure," he said, "a head of a fisherman, when I was sixteen years old.

"I THINK AN ARTIST'S CAPACITY TO HANDLE THE FIGURE IS A GREAT TEST OF HIS ABILITIES."

—WAYNE THIEBAUD

Wayne ran a risk. What if these new pictures weren't as good as his still lifes? What if Allan Stone, his gallery dealer, decided not to show them? But Wayne felt that he needed change in his work to keep it fresh.

At first he tried drawing from memory, as he had with food. The results were terrible. "I just didn't know enough about the figure and still don't," he said. So Wayne decided to work from live models. He asked friends and members of his family to sit for him.

"I posed for Pop," remembered Paul. Wayne's drawing, *Paul Aged 5 Years* (page 56), shows his son perched on a rocking chair, trying hard to hold still. Paul said that Wayne had to draw quickly. "It was the fastest thing he ever did."

That same year, 1965, Wayne started a portrait of his wife titled *Betty Jean Thiebaud & Book*. He worked on the painting for four years. "Mom modeled for Pop," recalled Paul. "He drew her from life." If Wayne worked on a painting of another woman and she wasn't there when he was finishing, he asked his wife to pose. He wound up putting his wife's face on other models' bodies. One of Wayne's best-known portraits, *Girl with Ice Cream Cone*, combines two of his favorite subjects: his wife and ice cream. Years later, he painted a group of five *Family Figures* (page 98). In it, his wife sits on the beach surrounded by their grown sons, Paul and Matt, and their wives.

BETTY JEAN THIEBAUD & BOOK, 1965–1969, OIL ON CANVAS, 36 X 30 INCHES,
COLLECTION OF CROCKER ART MUSEUM, SACRAMENTO

TWO MAJORETTES, 1962, OIL ON CANVAS, 36 X 48 INCHES, COLLECTION OF PAUL LEBARON THIEBAUD

Sometimes Wayne composed a painting with two similar figures to see if he could create "spacial tension," or excitement, in repeated images. In *Two Majorettes*, for instance, baton twirlers march toward the viewer in bright sunlight. They seem identical. But they're not. Their faces and hairdos are different, and their steps are slightly out of sync. The painting has no background. A hair-thin line barely suggests the ground. Only the shadows the girls cast hold them in place.

Shadows are an important part of Wayne's work. He usually tries six or eight different shadow shapes to find the one that is just right. Shadows in Wayne's paintings and drawings are full of color. For him, the painterly problems are always the same, whether he is drawing cakes or cheerleaders or bunnies: How to compose the picture? How to use color and light?

When Allan Stone saw Wayne's new work featuring people, he loved it. In 1965 he gave Wayne a show called *Figures*. Yet Wayne still felt the need to improve. He began attending weekly drawing sessions in San Francisco. He and a few fellow artists hired models to pose for them as they continued studying the human form, just like any other art students.

Of course, the most available model for Wayne would always be himself. "Almost every morning, when I get up," he said, "I've done a linear drawing of myself, for just five or ten minutes. I have this big stack of them, mostly just my head looking in the mirror." Wayne felt more comfortable using himself as the model because he didn't care how he looked in the picture. Occasionally he developed a sketch into a painting.

In *Self-Portrait with Suspenders* he seems cheerful. His head tilts slightly to one side as he peers through his glasses at his reflection. Is he judging his own work? Or is he thinking up a new painting challenge to set for himself?

SELF-PORTRAIT WITH SUSPENDERS, 1987, OIL ON CANVAS, 16 X 20 INCHES, THIEBAUD FAMILY COLLECTION

FROM FARMS TO "FANTASY CITY"

TOWARDS 280, 1999-2000, ACRYLIC AND OIL ON CANVAS, 54 X 60 INCHES, COURTESY OF LEBARON'S FINE ART, SACRAMENTO

DELTA, 1998, PASTEL ON PAPER, 31¼ X 22⅝ INCHES, PRIVATE COLLECTION

In the late 1960s Wayne tackled a familiar subject—landscapes—in a new way. He had always loved the look of the area where he lived, the Sacramento River Delta. "The Delta is full of these marvelous changes," he said. Seasons, colors, and crops. The patterns of the planted fields charmed him. But Wayne wanted to avoid the danger of simply painting pretty pictures. That would be too ordinary. Instead he wanted to show what he calls the "many ways of seeing the landscape in the same picture." How could he do that?

"I TRIED TO STEAL EVERY KIND OF IDEA—WESTERN, EASTERN—AND THE USE OF EVERYTHING I COULD THINK OF. SIZE DIFFERENCES, COLOR DIFFERENCES . . . EXAGGERATION."

—WAYNE THIEBAUD

Wayne often went driving along the levees, the banks built up along the river. He went over rolling hills and past farm ponds. On the way he made little sketches and later worked them into thumbnails of the scene. "You can make eight or ten thumbnails which might give you clues as to how compositions can be determined," he explained. "This gives you a way of seeing very quickly perhaps how one kind of arrangement is better than another."

Then he would create paintings—maybe little paintings at first—on board or canvas or in watercolors. Or studies in charcoal and pastel.

In his studio, Wayne would change the scale of the sketches, blowing them up into larger pictures, sometimes as big as 4 feet by 5 feet like the painting *Highland River*. Or even bigger. But sometimes that didn't work. If he couldn't figure out how to make a particular scene or composition come out the way he wanted it to, he'd either save the sketches as suggestions for future projects or throw them away. "That's the joy and fun and challenge of trying to get something small into something large," he said.

HIGHLAND RIVER, 1997, OIL ON CANVAS, 48 X 60 INCHES, COURTESY OF LEBARON'S FINE ART, SACRAMENTO
Y RIVER, 1998, OIL ON CANVAS, 72 X 72 INCHES, PRIVATE COLLECTION, LAKE TAHOE

POND, 1996/2000, PASTEL ON PAPER, 11¼ X 16⅜ INCHES, COURTESY OF PAUL THIEBAUD GALLERY, SAN FRANCISCO

He also played around with perspective. In *Highland River* (page 75), the trees closer to the viewer are bigger than the ones farther away near the top of the painting. But in *Y River* (page 75) Wayne turns things around and makes the trees farther back bigger than the ones up front. So the whole picture seems flat. Wayne fooled around with viewpoint, too. His pastel called *Pond* and his painting *The Riverhouse* (page 18) show the scenes as though he's seeing them from a spot on the ground. The pictures include the horizon line where earth meets sky. *Pond* even has a cow. Wayne remembered his father's and grandfather's farms as he did these pictures. Boyhood memories that he had stored came back to him.

Sometimes Wayne composed the scenes of farms and rivers from a totally different viewpoint above the ground. *Reservoir and Orchard* (page 31) and *Highland River* appear to be glimpsed from an airplane. Wayne dared to try anything to make his pictures exciting. Inspired by French artists like Henri Matisse and Pierre Bonnard, he painted with glorious colors—colors that created their own light. The vivid yellow and soft lavender of farmland and the peach tone of the water in *Reservoir and Orchard* are just as beautiful in their own way as any true colors found in nature.

While Wayne continued to work on landscapes and river-scapes, he took on yet another new challenge: cityscapes.

In 1973 he bought a second home in San Francisco on Potrero Hill, and he began making drawings and paintings of the neighborhood. The steep hills in San Francisco thrilled him. "I was . . . fascinated by those plunging streets, where you get down to an intersection and all four streets take off in different directions," he said. "You look at a hill and [it is so steep] it doesn't look as if the cars would be able to stay on it." His painting *24ᵗʰ Street Intersection* shows just such a car zooming down a hill to the right and looking as though it's just about to fall off the edge of the canvas. In the center of the painting a truck and another car in the distance swoop straight down toward the viewer at a frightening angle.

One day when Wayne first started his series of cityscapes he brought his easel out with him, set it up, and painted his picture right on the street. But Wayne felt that this realistic work was not successful. "I knew that I was in trouble," he said. Painting scenes just as they looked did not get across the scary feeling he wanted to convey.

24TH STREET INTERSECTION, 1977, OIL ON CANVAS, 35⅝ X 48 INCHES, PRIVATE COLLECTION

HOLLY PARK RIDGE, 1984, CHARCOAL ON PAPER, 22½ X 18¼ INCHES, PRIVATE COLLECTION

So he changed his method. "I went back in the studio, and began to make a lot of drawings with graphite or char-coal on paper, which I could move around a lot, kind of playing around with them. . . . San Francisco is a fantasy city. It's easy to make it into a pretend city, a kind of fairy tale."

Wayne made many sketches. "Sometimes those prove to be interesting enough to show," he said. "Mostly they just have to be destroyed." But he kept *Holly Park Ridge*. The drawing shows a dramatic view looking down on the tops of tall buildings and trees lining steep streets that seem to go straight up in the air. A diagonal shape representing a road plunges through the composition from the right side to the lower left corner. It sweeps down like a skateboard ramp.

Wayne even got a telescope. When he looked through it he discovered new ways of viewing city scenes that gave him ideas for paintings.

"YOU HAVE TO TAKE SOME CHANCES."

—WAYNE THIEBAUD

CAT & BUILDING, 1993, ACRYLIC ON CANVAS, 30 X 24 INCHES, PRIVATE COLLECTION

Just as he did with the landscapes, he changed the scale of his drawings and made little sketches into enormous paintings. He took pieces of drawings and paintings he had been working on and made new drawings, erasing a lot, and "moving things around. And suddenly," he said, "I began to get something which was more like the feel of the city that I'd been looking for."

Sometimes he added things that weren't really there to contrast the indoors with the outdoors. In *Cat & Building*, for instance, a cat that he painted from his imagination sits on a ledge and looks through a window at a skyscraper across the way. The cat, which is inside, seems calm and comfortable. Yet the viewer feels jittery and off-balance because the cat's perch is obviously so high up. What if the window opens and the cat jumps out? Windows surrounding the cat show nothing but sky and a tall building to the right. Repeated vertical lines of the skyscraper and windowpanes intensify the feeling of dizzying height. People have asked him if he suffers from vertigo—the sensation of tilting or falling even when standing still—as he does these paintings.

Dark City portrays San Francisco at night. Tall skyscrapers painted in deep shades of purple and periwinkle blue create a mood of excitement. The colors, though not true to life, give the feeling of nighttime. Little dabs of yellow and red suggest lit windows, street lamps, and cars driving up and down a hill that seems to go straight up into the air. The painting is huge—over 6 feet high—and is all verticals. Even the steep hill rising up in the middle like a roller coaster is shaped like the rectangular buildings on either side.

In this painting Wayne used the idea of caricature that he had learned from cartooning. He exaggerated. He made the hills steeper than they actually are, and he painted them in brighter colors in order "to get the feeling of things."

This time he faced the danger of overdoing it. If he made those hilly streets look too ridiculously steep, they might seem like something out of a fantasy or a dream. Wayne said to himself, "I've got to make sure somehow that all that greasiness, oiliness, tarriness, all the filth of the city is there as well as these shiny, bright, brassy diamond-like things."

DARK CITY, 1999, OIL ON CANVAS, 72¹⁄₈ X 54⁵⁄₈ INCHES, COURTESY OF LEBARON'S FINE ART, SACRAMENTO

URBAN FREEWAYS (STUDY), 1979-1980, OIL ON CANVAS, 24 X 20 INCHES, PRIVATE COLLECTION

Cars, traffic, and roadways also captured Wayne's interest as subjects for painting. Once again, his childhood memories influenced his work. "My uncle [Lowell] was a road maker," he recalled, "and when I was about eight years old, he gave me a little toy bulldozer and scraper and cars, and invited me to go and make this little world out in the backyard. . . . I had this earth place where I could make roads, tunnels, little buildings, and trees."

Urban Freeways (Study), painted in cheery colors, has the humorous quality of a cartoon. The maze of looping freeways reminded Wayne of Los Angeles, but he based the painting on a sketch he did in San Francisco. And his painting *Towards 280* (page 70) shows a "river of traffic" winding through the city. He could walk out his front door and cross over a freeway and see something very similar. "It's very spooky," he said, "what comes hurtling through there."

During the past 40 years Wayne has continued to work with cityscapes and landscapes. He sees them as research problems. Yet over and over, he keeps returning to his first love: desserts.

LOVABLE CAKES

CELEBRATION CAKES, 1992, PASTEL ON PAPER, 30 X 22 INCHES, PRIVATE COLLECTION

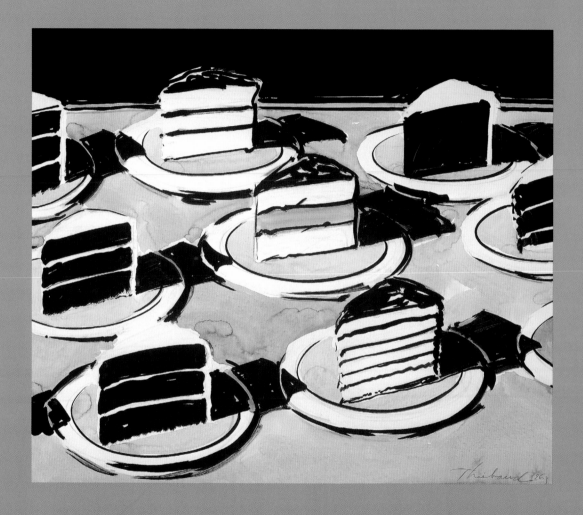

CAKE SLICES, 1963, WATERCOLOR ON PAPER, 20½ X 24½ INCHES, PRIVATE COLLECTION

What more could Wayne do with paintings of desserts? Plenty.

"ALMOST EVERYTHING I'VE DONE I'LL GO BACK TO AND DO AGAIN."

—WAYNE THIEBAUD

But with each picture he does something new. Sometimes he makes "slight differences" in the composition, like arranging cakes vertically instead of horizontally. Or making them big in relation to the size of the paper or canvas.

"I'LL SEE SOME BAKERY COUNTER . . . AND I THINK, I'D LIKE TO TRY THAT."

—WAYNE THIEBAUD

Celebration Cakes, a pastel, shows a display of cakes decorated for festive occasions.

The endless row of cakes running off the edge of the paper suggests that there's no limit to the special events for people to celebrate. One cake reads "Feliz Compli" the beginning of "Happy Birthday" in Spanish. Another says "Bon Cha—," starting "Good Luck" in French. And there's an old favorite of Wayne's, a cake with a valentine heart piped in frosting along with the word "Congratulations." Wayne signed this picture as he often does with a small heart before his last name.

"It's a little upside-down *W*," Wayne explained. It's also meant as a heart for good luck.

CELEBRATION CAKES, 1992, PASTEL ON PAPER, 30 X 22 INCHES, PRIVATE COLLECTION

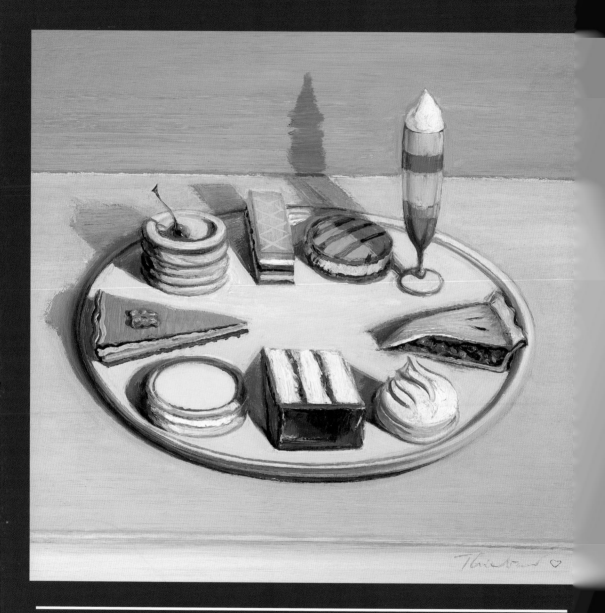

PARTY TRAY, 1994, OIL ON PANEL, 20 X 22 INCHES, PRIVATE COLLECTION, COURTESY OF LEBARON'S FINE ART, SACRAMENTO

Sometimes Wayne gives himself a new challenge by increasing the number of desserts in a picture. *Party Tray*, for instance, painted in oil, features a round mint-green tray of goodies centered on a square lavender background. The luscious assortment includes a piece of cherry pie, a slice of cake, an ice-cream parfait, a lemon tart, a Napoleon, and a meringue puff.

Dessert Table offers even more treats: 34! There are dishes of ice cream, plates of doughnuts, pieces of layer cake, frosted gingerbread squares, and a surprise—slices of juicy, red watermelon. The servings are lined up in parallel rows just like in a cafeteria. The canvas measures 4 feet by 5 feet.

All of these pictures share something besides sweets. In each picture, Wayne continues to solve painterly problems. How to portray desserts as geometric shapes? Equally important are the spaces between cakes and pastries on the tray. Wayne pays attention to the shadows cast by every parfait and piece of watermelon. The difference between objects and their shadows particularly interests him. "The object sort of stays," he said, "but the shadow can be long or not there at all." Color flows throughout and adds to the pleasure of the pictures.

When his students ask, "What do you think *I* ought to be painting?" Wayne says,

"FIND SOMETHING YOU WANT TO PAINT. SOMETHING YOU REALLY LOVE."

However, when his son Paul was about eight or ten years old and asked for "regular drawing lessons" with a few of his friends, Wayne gave them assignments. "I had them do drawing problems," he recalled. "Drawing an object with light and shade, getting a three-dimensional world to a two-dimensional surface." Wayne corrected the children's drawings and told them to keep sketchbooks.

"Pop had us draw from a very young age," remembered Paul. "We drew that box," he said, pointing to a box of Kleenex tissues, "for a solid year. We continued to make it almost photo-realistic."

CHEESE SLICES, 1986, OIL ON CANVAS, 20 X 30 INCHES, COLLECTION OF PAUL LEBARON THIEBAUD

FAMILY FIGURES, 1990, OIL ON BOARD, 11⅞ X 15½ INCHES, THIEBAUD FAMILY COLLECTION

All the Thiebaud children have been exposed to art. Paul is a collector and art dealer, his brother, Matt, is a painter, their sister Twinka is a painter and used to model for artists, and Mallary works at painting, too.

Wayne believes that everyone should draw and paint:

"PAINTING AND DRAWING IS SOMETHING YOU CAN ENJOY WITHOUT IT HAVING TO BE ART OR WORRYING ABOUT IT BEING ART. . . . EVERYBODY SHOULD HAVE THAT PRIVILEGE AND THAT GREAT WAY OF KNOWING THINGS."

In 1990 Wayne retired from teaching full-time at University of California, Davis. As an emeritus professor he now teaches studio art and art history part-time. "Since I'm working for nothing they can't fire me," he joked.

Wayne has received dozens of medals, awards, and honorary degrees for both his teaching and painting. His work is exhibited all over the world. On the occasion of his eightieth birthday, the Fine Arts Museums of San Francisco organized a huge retrospective of his work from the first row of pies to a Goofy doll painted on a box for Paul. The show opened at the Legion of Honor in San Francisco and then traveled to Fort Worth, Texas, and Washington, D.C., winding up at the Whitney Museum of American Art in New York City. But the tribute that probably means the most to Wayne is the way his son Paul lovingly shows his paintings and drawings in the Sacramento gallery.

Even at the age of 86, Wayne still paints in his studio every day (and plays tennis, his other great passion, a couple of times a week).

"PAINTING IS LIFE FOR ME. IT IS A KIND OF MIRACLE."

—WAYNE THIEBAUD

CANDY APPLES, 1989, WATERCOLOR OVER MONOTYPE, 8 X 8 INCHES, PRIVATE COLLECTION, COURTESY OF ALLAN STONE GALLERY, NEW YORK

JOLLY CONES, 2002, OIL ON BOARD, 11 X 8½ INCHES, PRIVATE COLLECTION

In spite of his enormous success and the many honors heaped upon him, Wayne remains modest. "I think of myself as a beginner. Sometimes that's the whole joy. If you could just do it, there'd be no point in doing it.

"I DON'T THINK I'VE EVER PAINTED A PICTURE I REALLY FELT TOO SATISFIED WITH. IT'S ALWAYS THE NEXT PICTURE THAT KEEPS YOU GOING."

As recently as 2002 Wayne painted *Jolly Cones*, a pair of upside-down ice-cream cones with "happy faces." The silly cones sum up the spirit of Wayne's art—his sense of fun, his love of color, and his joy in painting happy pictures. Delicious.

Materials marked with an asterisk (*) are suitable for younger readers.

Books

de Kooning: An American Master.
Stevens, Mark and Annalyn Swan.
New York: Afred A. Knopf, 2004.

*Vision and Revision: Hand Colored Prints by Wayne Thiebaud.
Introduction by Wayne Thiebaud.
San Francisco: Chronicle Books, 1991.

Wayne Thiebaud.
Tsujimoto, Karen.
San Francisco and Seattle: University of Washington Press and the San Francisco Museum of Modern Art, 1985.

Wayne Thiebaud: A Paintings Retrospective.
Nash, Steven A. and Adam Gopnik.
San Francisco: Fine Arts Museums of San Francisco with Thames & Hudson, 2000.

Catalogs

Wayne Thiebaud.
Coplans, John.
Pasadena: Pasadena Art Museum, 1968.

Thiebaud Collects Thiebaud.
McGough, Stephen C.
Sacramento: Crocker Art Museum, 1996.

*Wayne Thiebaud: Pastels, 1960–2000.
Introduction by Paul LeBaron Thiebaud.
San Francisco: Campbell-Thiebaud Gallery, 2000.

Wayne Thiebaud: Figurative Works, 1959–1994.
Introduction and Acknowledgments by Charles Strong, Curator of the Exhibition.
The Wiegand Gallery, College of Notre Dame in cooperation with the
Northern Arizona Art Museum and Galleries, 1994.

*Wayne Thiebaud: Cityscapes.
November 9–December 18, 1993.
San Francisco: Campbell-Thiebaud Gallery, 1993.

Catalogs (continued)

*Wayne Thiebaud: Landscapes.
November 11–December 20, 1997.
San Francisco: Campbell-Thiebaud Gallery, 1997.

*Wayne Thiebaud: Riverscapes, 2002.
San Francisco, New York, and London:
Paul Thiebaud Gallery, Allan Stone Gallery, and Faggionato Fine Arts, 2002.

*Wayne Thiebaud: Fifty Years of Painting.
Foreword by Dana Self.
Kansas City, Missouri: Kemper Museum of Contemporary Art, 2003.

Wayne Thiebaud: Works from 1955 to 2003.
Malibu and Sacramento: Frederick R. Weisman Museum of Art,
Pepperdine University and University Library Gallery, California State University, Sacramento, 2003.

Wayne Thiebaud at Allan Stone Gallery: Celebrating 33 Years Together.
New York: Allan Stone Gallery, 1994

Periodicals

View: Interview with Wayne Thiebaud by Constance Lewallen.
San Francisco: Point Publications, Winter 1990.

Articles

"California Classroom: A Learning Link to the Norton Simon Museum."
Los Angeles Times, November 13, 2000.

Cheng, Scarlet.
"A Life Rich in Possibilities."
Los Angeles Times, Saturday, January 18, 2003.

Cohen, David.
"High Cholesterol Nonedibles."
New York Sun, Arts & Letters, Thursday, April 7, 2005.

Fabricant, Florence.
"At the Whitney, Cake Imitates Art."
New York Times, August 1, 2001.

Articles (continued)

Kimmelman, Michael.
"Wistful Joy in Soda-Fountain Dreams."
New York Times, Friday, June 29, 2001

Pagel, David.
"Unconventional Confections."
Los Angeles Times, January 2003.

Schrambling, Regina.
"The Man Who Paints Pies Knows the Real Thing, Too."
New York Times, Wednesday, June 27, 2001

Public Lectures

Conversations with Wayne Thiebaud and Wendy Lesser,
Founding Editor of *The Threepenny Review*, Herbst Theatre, San Francisco, April 20, 2005.

Interviews Conducted by the Author in Person or via Telephone

Allan Stone, June 10, 2005.

Wayne Thiebaud, April 11, 2005.

Paul LeBaron Thiebaud, April 11, 2005.

Cassette tape recording by Wayne Thiebaud for author, April 29, 2005.

Index
Page numbers in italic refer to photographs.